A SHORT HISTORY OF

ALBANIA

AND THE ALBANIAN PEOPLE

Nicolae Iorga

A SHORT HISTORY OF
A⅃BANIA
AND THE ALBANIAN PEOPLE

Introduction by A.K. Brackob
Translated by Bernard Gibbons

HISTRIA
ACADEMIC

Histria Academic

Las Vegas ◊ Chicago ◊ Palm Beach

Published in the United States of America by
Histria Books
7181 N. Hualapai Way, Suite 130-86
Las Vegas, NV 89166 USA
HistriaBooks.com

Histria Academic is an imprint of Histria Books. Titles published under the imprints of Histria Books are exclusively distributed worldwide.

Library of Congress Control Number: 2024931012

ISBN 978-1-59211-421-4 (hardcover)
ISBN 978-1-59211-438-2 (eBook)

Contents

Introduction..7

Author's Preface 11

I — Origins 13

II — The Albanians and Byzantium............................21

III — First Albanian Historic Manifestations.............24

IV — The Albanians and the Crusade.........................31

V — The Albanians and the Angevins of Naples..........38

VI — Albanian expansion at the end of the Middle Ages.....................43

VII — Albanian States 47

VIII — Scanderbeg...54

IX — After Scanderbeg: Suffering and Revolts............62

X — Albania in the Service of the Turks.....................67

XI — Albanian renewal...75

Appendix Extracts from Ottoman official statistics.............79

Suggested Reading 81

INTRODUCTION

A Short History of Albania and the Albanian People by Nicolae Iorga stands as one of the earliest comprehensive attempts to trace the history of the Albanian people from their origins to the early twentieth century. Originally published in French in 1919, the book introduced a Western audience to the history of a little-known yet fascinating land at a pivotal moment in European history.

Nicolae Iorga wrote this small book at the end of World War I, a period marked by significant geopolitical upheaval. The Treaty of Versailles, which would reshape the map of Europe, was being signed, and Iorga sought to make a compelling case for the recognition of Albania, a nation that had only declared its independence from the Ottoman Empire seven years earlier. Iorga is often regarded today as a cultural nationalist, using culture and history to legitimize national claims and foster a sense of identity.

According to his biographer, Nicholas M. Nagy-Talavera, Iorga perceived "Albania as a kind of 'balcony on the Venetian Sea,' (the Adriatic Sea). Whatever sympathy Iorga felt toward Italy, he always recognized that the long eastern shore of the Adriatic is inhabited by Slavs and Albanians, who are most unhappy about Italian pretensions."[1] This perspective highlights Iorga's nuanced understanding of regional dynamics and his advocacy for the Albanian people.

---

[1] Nicholas M. Nagy-Talavera, Nicolae Iorga: A Biography. Palm Beach: Center for Romanian Studies, 2022, p. 325.

Nicolae Iorga was one of the most eminent historians of the twentieth century. Born in Botoșani, Romania, on June 5, 1871 (old style), he pursued his education at the University of Iași, Romania's cultural capital, before furthering his studies in Paris, Berlin, and Leipzig, where he earned his doctorate in 1893. Over his lifetime, Iorga published more than 1,000 books and 12,000 articles, making him one of the most prolific historians in world history.

While Iorga is best known for his extensive work on Romanian history, he was an erudite scholar who produced a wide range of works covering various aspects of European history, including masterful studies on the Byzantine[2] and Ottoman Empires. His scholarship was characterized by its breadth and depth, reflecting a profound commitment to understanding and documenting the past.

Iorga's interest in Albania was not solely academic; he had a personal connection as well. His family had emigrated to the Principality of Moldavia from Greece in the early 1700s. The earliest recorded mention of his ancestral name was Galeongiul, suggesting Albanian roots. This personal link may have fueled his interest in Albanian history and culture. Active in Romanian politics, Iorga sometimes faced derisive remarks from political opponents who would refer to him as an Albanian, underscoring his perceived connection to the Albanian people.

Despite these personal connections, Iorga remained a steadfast Romanian patriot. His sympathy for the Albanian past was largely rooted in its Thracian origins. Iorga sought to explore the connections between the Romanian and Albanian peoples, emphasizing

---

[2] Nicolae Iorga, *The Byzantine Empire*. Palm Beach: Histria Academic, 2024.

their shared Thraco-Illyrian heritage. This common ancestry is reflected in certain words unique to both languages. During the late 1930s, before the Italian invasion of Albania, Iorga even attempted to establish an institute in Albania dedicated to studying these ancient connections.

Available in English for the first time, Nicolae Iorga's *A Short History of Albania and the Albanian People* is significant both as a work of cultural nationalism and as an early scholarly effort to outline the history of Albania. Iorga's work helped define the Albanian nation, providing a historical framework that legitimized its national claims. His scholarship offered a detailed account of Albania's past, from its ancient Thraco-Illyrian roots to its struggles for independence in the early twentieth century.

Iorga's book serves as a testament to the enduring relevance of history in shaping national identities and fostering cultural understanding. By tracing the historical trajectory of the Albanian people, Iorga highlighted the resilience and continuity of a nation that had long been overshadowed by more dominant regional powers. His work underscores the importance of historical scholarship in giving voice to marginalized and overlooked communities, offering them a place in the broader tapestry of human history.

Nicolae Iorga's *A Short History of Albania and the Albanian People* remains a foundational text in the study of Albanian history. Written at a critical juncture in European history, the book provides a comprehensive and sympathetic account of the Albanian people's journey through time. Iorga's dual role as a cultural nationalist and a rigorous historian allowed him to craft a narrative that both legitimized Albanian national claims and contributed to the broader understanding of European history.

The availability of this work in English opens new avenues for appreciating Iorga's scholarship and the rich history of Albania. It serves as a reminder of the power of historical narratives in shaping our understanding of the past and informing our present. Through Iorga's meticulous research and profound insights, readers gain a deeper appreciation of Albania's unique heritage and its place in the world.

A.K. Brackob

AUTHOR'S PREFACE

At a time when the Albanian question is again posed and when the representatives of the oldest people — along with the Basques — in all of Europe ask that their right is recognized to a homeland, which they hope to lead in the direction imposed by the postulates of modern civilization, at a time when Italy — which very much has the right to do so — takes an interest in the fate of its half-brothers in the Balkans, I have been asked to provide a summary of the history of this old and tragic Albania.

In 1913, I taught some lessons on Albanian history for a whole year at the Institute for the Study of Southeastern Europe in Bucharest. I had not yet had the chance to publish the Romanian text, which had been typed up.

These lessons have served as the basis for the slim volume presented here, not for the experts, who know nearly everything which is contained in these pages, but for a public — today assessing political processes — to which the new scientific data, enriched very recently by abundant information, has not yet been revealed.[3]

I hope that, by these submissions, this book will serve the cause of national justice and that, which is so closely linked to it, of civilization itself — each nation having its place in the spiritual and material life of the whole of humanity.

Nicolae Iorga

---

[3] We will indicate the *Illyrisch-Albanische Forschungen*, Munich-Leipzig 1916, where Jan Thaldezy has brought together some articles of great importance and the recent studies by Messrs. Sufday and Szegh, in the *Ungarische Rundschau* of 1916, volume 1.

1
ORIGINS

The preface to the collection of deeds and regesta relating to Albania which three very erudite Austro-Hungarians, Messrs. Jireček, Thalloczy and Šufflay, began to publish some years ago, attempts a definition of Albania.[4] This definition would have made little sense to an Albanian of the old generation, attached above all to his gens or clan.

Undoubtedly, from the viewpoint of language, as much as race, we can distinguish the limits of habitation of an Albanian nation, while from the viewpoint of certain historic memories, there also exists a common consciousness, superior to that of clans. In terms of dialogue, the Ghegs in the north and the Tosks in the south have long been distinguished. Old traditional names, like that of the Malissores or the Mirdites, have been kept until today. We can also attempt a grammar of the Gheg dialect and the Tosk dialect, considered in their specific individuality, but a history of the Northern group differentiated from that of the Southern group is as impossible, in anything other than a purely local sense, as that of a history of the Malissores and Mirdites.

And yet, when we wish to fix the borders of historic Albania, we come up against, beyond the difficulty caused by migrations and the invasive rivalry of races on the same territory, and the fact that this

---

[4] *Acta et diplomata res Albaniae mediae aetatis illustrantia*, 1, Vienna 1913.

Albania which has for some time tried to reconstruct itself has never in the past existed as a single state, subject to the same single national authority.

The greatest hero of the race, Scanderbeg, the valiant chevalier of Christianity in the fifteenth century — and he had started out as a Muslim, whether through free choice or compulsion — had, beyond the sentiment of adherence to his family and his group, that of the political and religious mission which he fulfilled, but, disposing of elements of different nations, Albanians, Slavs, Greeks, Latin and Orthodox, he had no very clear consciousness of representing the long past and possible future of a nation.

However, from the viewpoint of the editors of these old documents concerning medieval Albania, the territorial limits are more or less indifferent. This is a people which, while being closely attached to its land, which it fiercely defended against any foreigner, often transcended its boundaries without seeking a new dispensation and without wishing to give a broader territorial basis to its existence. What is intriguing then is not this territory itself, whether broader or narrower, nor the towns, mostly belonging to foreigners, nor the villages scattered amongst rocks or lost in the mountain valleys, but rather the vitality of an admirable conserving energy and an astonishing strength of resistance, which forms the interest of the history of the Albanians and explains their current existence.

For some, the studies of philologists concerning the names of localities in the Balkan peninsula, as well as on the other side of the Adriatic Sea, up to the coastal region of the Tyrol, have succeeded in fixing the territory over which the old race of Illyrians, from whom today's Albanians are undoubtedly descended, extended. But the language whose elements can be recognized in the nomenclature of these regions has not been spoken for centuries — the descendants of the Illyrians have loaned to their brothers and cousins, to their more numerous and more advanced neighbors, living in fertile regions open to the outside world, a new dialect, that of the Thracians. The descendants of these Thracians came to speak Greek, Slav, or the Romance Latin of the Romanians today, whereas the Thracian language has remained the exclusive attribute of the Albanians, the Romanian language having retained only a very small group of words borrowed from the idiom of these ancestors.

The Thracian spoken by the Albanians is a terse, concise language of combat and command disdaining the harmony of vowels, letting harsh consonants clash as in an armed conflict. As there has been an influence of Latin, due to the political and military invasion of the Republic and of the Empire, significant infiltrations occurred in the cities along the coast, which became completely Roman. Latin elements penetrated into Albanian, and these elements are so numerous, broadly embracing all the notions of a higher civilization, that we can rightly consider Albanian as a semi-Romance language, though these words have undergone, in passing through the throats of rough Balkan warriors, modifications which give them the same abrupt aspect that forms the barbarous yet imposing character of this language. Turkish, Slavic, Greek and Italian words have then been added to this primitive base.

The Latin words that we find in the Albanian language do not however always cover, as is the case with Romanian and all the Romance languages, basic notions belonging to the cycle of nature, the human body, daily life and thought. The original Thracian basis indubitably forms the base of the language, in the same way that it is the basic element so far as race is concerned. The terms relating to the Christian religion can only be Latin because of the Western character that it has had from the beginning and which the new religious form was able to keep, despite Byzantine influences. Italian terms, Venetian nuances above all, are not lacking, as a consequence of the fact that the religion was later for centuries represented by missionaries, priests originating from the neighboring peninsula, and by Albanians who were their disciples.

The Latin basis of the Albanian language does not belong to the vulgar parlance, as we find it at the base of the Romance languages properly so called. It belongs to a more ancient and purer form of Latin. These words have mostly been borrowed, with corresponding notions, at the time when the Roman republic played on the Balkan side the same role played later in the same region by a conquering, colonizing Venice. The Greek historian of Republican Rome, Polybius, tells us in a very detailed manner about the wars waged by the legions against the Illyrian elements who posed a threat to navigation in the Adriatic Sea. The names of the queen Theuta and her husband, king Agron, ancestors of the Albanian chieftains of the Middle Ages and the modern era, are often found in the pages of the Greek historian of the Republic.

A little later, the Romans encountered, on this western side of the Balkan peninsula, other Illyrian enemies than the pirates of these ancient monarchs.

Macedonia fought under the successors of Alexander the Great for its independent existence. In relation to this kingdom, Hellenic only in terms of the civilization acquired by the dominant class, because the population was of the same Illyrian origin as that of the coast, chieftains of purely Illyric character appeared at different times in the development of the purely military organization of the Macedonians. This time it amounted very much to a political conflict with a force which was organized to a certain extent. Such was the meaning of the war that Rome waged against "King" Pleuratis, "King" Gentius, and, at the time of the Macedonian liquidation, the incursion into Italy of King Pyrrhus, whose elephants, introduced to the military system by the conqueror of Asia, would sometimes sow terror in the midst of the legions. This Pyrrhus, whose role has been a little exaggerated by Roman historians of a later epoch, desirous to aggrandize everything belonging to the past of their city, appears to us rather similar to these chieftains of the Stratioti, also bearing Greek names, who played a significant role as mercenaries in the Italian wars of the fifteenth and above all the sixteenth century. In his time, Pyrrhus had, like all these mercenaries of the early modern era, singers of his exploits, for in thought as in action, the Albanian taste for epics has continued from the most obscure centuries until the time when a clearer light is projected by modern sources.

Pyrrhus was a king, and by this very character of a military royalty leading his people to conquests without end and often without purpose, the Macedonians themselves proved their participation in the common life of the Thraco-Illyrian race. While serving under Philip, Alexander the Great, and his successors, they pursued an ideal of Hellenic revenge against Asia. These Macedonian warriors were linked together by a sentiment entirely other than that of the civic commu-

nity of the Greek municipal organizations, and this sentiment is undoubtedly not different from that which both Scanderbeg and Ali
Pasha gave to their superb warriors; it is that of personal faith and of
devotion to the chieftain, such as the Germans knew at the time of
the barbarian migrations.

Beyond the information provided by Polybius and Dio Cassius
and some mentions in the Latin writers of the same epoch, information is lacking concerning this Illyrian nucleus in the Balkans
which would later become the Albanian people. Of course, this does
not constitute an argument to conclude the non-existence at a certain
time of the primordial elements of this race or that the first Albanians
we encounter in the medieval era would have descended from regions
situated more to the North of the peninsula. As with the Romanians,
who lived between the abandonment of Dacia by Aurelian's legions
and the first mentions of Vlachs in Byzantine sources, the silence of
contemporary authors only proves the lack of interest toward this or
that people on the part of those who, in representing civilization, were
in a position to provide testimonies. The writers of ancient Rome had
no reason to interest themselves in the obscure doings of those who
inhabited the mountains of Albania, these *scopuli*, whose name, rather
than the Latin verb *excipio* ("I understand") lives in the Albanian national name of Shqiptars.

The history of the Roman provinces, which have existed on Albanian lands, do not concern in any way the development of the race.
It is entirely otherwise with the Slav invasion, which in the 6th century submerged this whole territory.

These Slavs destroyed almost completely the Roman element
found on the very shore of the sea. Certain cities disappeared. Others

experienced more or less long periods of slumber. The ruins of a city, which went under the transparent name of Captat, could be seen near Ragusa until very late in the Middle Ages A Roman dialect, distinct from that of Romanians, was formed on this coast and in the neighboring islands, whereas Romanian itself henceforth took on a fixed character in the valleys of the Pindus, throughout the hinterland of the Adriatic and also on the Danube and in the Carpathians.

From this Roman nucleus of Dalmatia there remains only insignificant debris of which the last survivors have become extinct, taking with them the language itself, in the island of Veglia.

This was the time of great displacements. The Illyrians, to whom the Romans probably already applied the name of Albanians (the sources cite a town called Albanopolis) were seemingly refugees faced with Latin civilization itself before seeking a new refuge faced with Slav barbarism, in the mountainous regions of the interior. This would have happened in the same way to these Dacians, of Thracian origin, who, after the conquest of their country by Trajan and the establishment of the Roman province, would not resign themselves to living under the new civilized regime and would live, mixed in with barbarians properly so called, in the neighborhood, as irreconcilable enemies, then as isolated incompatibles.

The Slav expansion was not everywhere the creator of a durable state of affairs. The existence of the Slavs in the Greek countries and until the base of the Peloponnese can only be recognized today by the names of localities of an easily recognizable character and perhaps by certain physical aspects of the current population. We find Slav names — not to speak of the ethnic note in the aspect of the current populations — on a part of Albanian territory. This does not in any way mean that the current Albanians are the descendants of Slav ancestors, but rather that after having been pushed aside for some time by an invasion which imposed on the country Slav colonists of a more or less transitory nature, the Albanians came back in a subsequent generation, having lost the of the former names of these localities which they could at last return to. The Slavs, who sought the riches of Constantinople, and all that the Adriatic coast could offer them, had no interest in maintaining their stay in these impoverished Pindus valleys which could only be loved by the tenacious soul of the aborigines.

II
THE ALBANIANS AND BYZANTIUM

The Eastern Roman empire, whose Byzantine Greek-speaking character became precise at the very epoch of the Slav invasions, never abandoned its rights to the dispute regions, at this time in history, between invaders and invaded, between Albanians and Slavs. But, under the religious relationship, the province of Illyricum kept its relations with the other Rome in the West, which had given it its first missionaries: that also meant adherence to the Latin civilization which was represented by this Western church.

The Pope for a long time had his representative in the Balkan peninsula in Salonika. From the beginning of the sixth century, Dyrrachium was the residence of a Metropolite, with the title of Epirus and Doclea. Before the era of the emperors Justin and Justinian, the true creator of Greek Byzantine, who tried to reconstitute to his advantage the old Roman unity, we already find Albanian bishops with Greek names: Theodule, Dynate, which did not yet mean either Hellenization or new links with this Greek Rome. But, from 512, Pope Symmachus was obliged to recall to obedience the head of the Church in Illyricum, Dardania and the two Dacias. The continuous struggle between the two influences took place over an indigenous population of which a part at least remained faithful to its language and traditions. The center of religious life moved during this same century to the Nicopolis of Epirus.

Whereas in 531 a bishop in Thessaly attended a Roman synod recognizing the rights of the Pope over Illyricum, Justinian soon succeeded in dealing a decisive blow to the influence the West continued to exert, undertaking the conquest of these eastern regions more closely linked to his crown. In 535 he elevated his hometown, located in the environs of Skopje or Üsküb, to the dignity of a great hierarchical center, giving it the name of Prima Justiniana.

However, Rome maintained its rights. As it had not abandoned the Danube castles, it continued to send its emissaries to islands like Meleda, which bordered the Adriatic coast of the Balkans. And it was Rome which fought the so-called "three chapters" heresy in these Dalmatian towns. We know that, in the ninth century, Pope Nicholas had a momentary illusion of being able to win to his Western church the Bulgar dynasty, which ended up recognizing the religious sovereignty of Constantinople.

But, as with these Bulgars, whose political relations tended towards Byzantium, the Slavs who inhabited the western regions of the Peninsula oriented their interests towards the same capital of the Eastern empire. Exercising hegemony over the regions still remaining free or autonomous, they essentially contributed to detaching them from Roman obedience. And, in fact, from 599, the bishops of Durazzo, Prima Justiniana, and Nicopolis convened at a Constantinople synod with there Eastern colleagues properly called.

The reintegration of the West in its former traditions of influence, which began only around the year 1000, was achieved through the Venetian Republic. Without the prestige and strength of the Doges, Albania would never have been detached from Constantinople: the very character of the race would have been affected, and it would have perhaps been confused with the surrounding Slavs and Greeks, against the orthodox character, which fought for centuries, conserving nationality itself, the action of missionaries coming from the West.

In 691, the bishop of Durazzo signed a synodal act in Constantinople. By 787, Durazzo was completely Greek. And as, during this same century, the Byzantine emperors began their heated struggle against the cult of images, considering the iconodules of Rome as heretics, the separation between the two Churches became more marked, and the agents of the Empire had one more motive to severely forbid any relations with the former spiritual heads of the Albanian regions. It was in vain that Pope Nicholas, trying to resume, thanks also to open support, the old traditions of domination, tried to win over the Balkans through the emissaries he sent to the court of the Bulgar Tsar Boris.

III
FIRST ALBANIAN HISTORIC MANIFESTATIONS

Throughout this time, not a single source speaks to us of the existence, slow development, or political progress of the Albanian race, now closely linked to the Greek Byzantium of Constantinople or to the Bulgar Byzantium of Preslave — since, in one case and the other, whatever the race of these dynasties, their advisors, and their warriors, it only amounted to the Roman imperial idea in the East. However, there was a development, and we can indeed note the results of it by this imperial creation of revolt, of separation, which took place towards the end of the tenth century in the regions where the old and new masters were the two nationalities, until then forgotten and neglected, the Albanians and the Romanian Vlachs.

Following long fruitless efforts to conquer and dominate the capital of eastern Romanism, the self-styled Bulgarian Empire succumbed to the blows of the Byzantine Caesars and their Russian auxiliaries. Byzantine domination extended to the Danube. But soon a new Tsarate emerged in the area of Ohrid, claiming, under chieftains of Bulgarian nationality, continuity with the state that had just fallen in Preslav.

But the whole character of this new foundation, its struggles against the Empire, the incidents of its short existence, in no way manifested the characteristic traits of Bulgaria so long definitively destroyed, but rather that of the Albanian-Vlach inhabitants of the mountains of Pindus. Their raids extended, for some years, from one end of the peninsula to another. Tsar Samuel and his weak successors, who still opposed the efforts of Basil II, the "Bulgar slayer," employed the fresh forces of the new races for a Byzantine imperial ideal, in relation to the old Bulgar opposition to Greece.

When Basil's soldiers scored a definitive victory, these regions, where the aboriginal population had been deployed in the service of these foreign masters, were subjected to the authority of the Byzantine duke of Durazzo. Once again, as this Empire of the eleventh century undoubtedly had a Greek national character, Albania — with the territories inhabited by these Vlachs, who enjoyed in the eleventh century, as is well shown by a Byzantine source of this epoch of an administrative and military character, an autonomous organization in Thessaly, under the hereditary chieftains of their nation — was exposed to the danger of being confused with the dominant Hellenism. It was a new intervention, at this time by the Normans, coming from the Kingdom of the Two Sicilies, and the Venetians, that conserved these two interesting races in the Balkans.

By the chivalrous rise of the Italian Normans and by the economic expansion of Venice, now almost completely escaped from Byzantine suzerainty, Albania was resuscitated. Finding itself henceforth at the point of intersection of the trends of domination, this territory and the people who lived there gained for the first time a great interest of universal history, and we can pursue the story of the land and the progress of the race.

Byzantine domination was based on the military relationship on Durazzo, at the head of which was the duke, a *hypatos*, a *sebastos*, one

of the main dignitaries of the Empire, and, under the religious relationship of the city of Ochrida, located in the interior, where the
archbishop resided, a Greek dependent of the Patriarch of Constantinople. In Durazzo, Jean Ducas, brother in law of the emperor Alexis
Comnène, then a Comnène nephew of the emperor, Jean, succeeded
each other at the head of the imperial administration. At the time of
the first crusade we also find, commanding the Byzantine fleet in the
Adriatic Sea, an admiral, Maurocatalon. In Ochrida, we see as head
of the Greek or Greek-influenced clergy an archbishop of the intel-
lectual distinction and talent of Theophylact, whose writings dominate the literary works of the Byzantines at the beginning of the
twelfth century. The province was also governed in the north by another Byzantine dignitary, residing in Skopje, to defend the frontiers
against the movements of the Slavs of the interior, the Serbs. And a
very complete religious organization covered all this Albanian territory, with bishops resident in Prizrend, Castoria, and Belgrade on the
Adriatic Sea, what is today Berat. Another bishop resided in Dibra,
and his successors would finally establish themselves in Kitschevo.

But towards the end of the eleventh century a western offensive
was directed against this province of Greek Arbanon (Arbanon was
first a city, then a province: Raban, in Slav),whose results could not
be dismissed throughout the subsequent era.

It is also represented by the new Serbian state which formed on
the coast of the Adriatic. At the beginning, this was the Croat branch
which, having founded a kingdom on the Save and the Drave, extended its domination well into the Balkan peninsula and up to the
coast of the Adriatic Sea. The heritage of the Croat sovereigns, the

dominators of Dalmatia, was however taken on, inasmuch as the dynasty became extinct, by the Magyars, whose King Coloman had himself crowned in the maritime city of Belgrade. This did not, however, prevent the Serbs from taking on the work of Slav royal organization a little lower in the same regions. And they were part of the Roman Seat, which had supported the Croats and had created the apostolic royalty of the Hungarians, a powerful and continuous support. The Voivodes, the Cnèzes, the Serb župans, were all the heirs of this Croat force to which they had been subject and consequently they would recognize this Western influence without which the Croat state itself would never have existed. Again, the West came to the rescue to render to the indigenous races their most ancient religious and political relations.

In 1070, the Serb chieftain on the coast of the Adriatic, Michel, addressed the Pope to ask from him the royal crown which had previously belonged to the Croat Svonimir; at the same time, as there could not be a king without a metropolitan archbishop, Michel wished to obtain this title for the head of his Church, residing no longer in Antivari, the former hierarchical center, but in Ragusa.

So as not the offend the Magyar kings, the Holy Seat refused the royal title to the first Michel, then to his successor Bodin, and finally to Michel, the son of Bodin. This did not stop them from calling themselves kings, not of the Serbs only, but of the Slavs in general, "reges Slavorum."

But as the supposedly Bulgar Tzarat of Ochrida based itself on Albanian and Vlach forces, Albanian and Romanian Vlach support was absolutely necessary for the maintenance of this Serbian royalty, still exposed to the revenge of the Byzantines. De facto, the state founded on the shores of the Adriatic, with a Catholic church and an influence of Western art, had a Slav-Byzantine character, from every point comparable to what can be noted, with a much greater wealth of information , in the fifteenth century for the princes with Greek names of Avlona (Vlorë). For the rest, when they were not kings of the Slavs in their deeds, these dynasts took the title of the former Duklja, without national character; in 1090, the archbishop was also that of Duklja, having under his authority Antivari itself and the convents of the "Dalmatins, as well as the Greeks and the Slavs ("*tam Dalmatinorum, quam Grecorum atque Selavorum*"), and there is no doubt about the true national note of these "Dalmatins" who were neither Serbs nor Greeks. There was also a monastery, where the kings came to reside, near Scutari, amid the most characteristic Albanian population, that of Saints Sergius and Bacchus, where the tomb of the princes was located.

While these Serbs extended a Catholic Western influence, Latin and thus Italian, over the Albanians, the Italians themselves came to interfere in the affairs of the peninsula. The first crusade brought the chiefs of the Normans to Durazzo, and the Greeks of the emperor Alexis had to fight the knights of prince Bohemond, whose intention was to submit this empire of Byzantium which seemed only to be able to revive in a new form, imposed by the Westerners. For a long time, the Norman royalty of the Two Sicilies desired possession of Byzantium, and it would take very little to achieve its ends by employing the immense Christian migration towards the Holy Places.

Byzantium escaped this danger but from 1070 this Venetian fleet, which the old Byzantine emperors considered as belonging to them and which could be employed to safeguard their domination in the

Adriatic Sea, was fighting the intrusive Norman fleet. This time the Doge defended the interests of the emperor, who he considered as his master. He also defended the Ionian islands against another attempt from the same Normans. In exchange, by a great imperial privilege, the Venetians obtained the right to trade throughout all Albania as far as the town of Canina and further still, towards the Greek countries. From 1072, however, the Venetians, envied for their wealth, were forced to quit the territory of the Empire, and before the movement of the crusade, in which they participated, these republicans from eastern Italy attacked the possessions of the Caesar. A century later, after repeated efforts to have the heritage of the Croats in Dalmatia, against the king of Hungary, they seized Zara, the capital of the province, by the arms of another surge of the crusade.

Byzantium resumed its former situation, although only for a few decades, under Manuel Conmène. At a time when Rascian Serbia was invaded by the Greek legions, penetrating though the Romanian forests towards Galicia, where Ancona itself, Italy's gateway to the West, was occupied by an imperial garrison, the Albanians returned entirely under the administration of the Byzantine duke of Durazzo.

There was a new Byzantine duchy in Niche, another in Castoria; Dalmatia and Duklja formed the duchy territory of a certain Isaac, a dependent of that emperor Manuel who a Latin contemporary characterized as "very pious and always triumphant". Already the abbots of "Sanctus Salvator Arbanensis", Lazare, the bishop of the Albanians (*Albanorum*), the "Arbanenis" prayer began to bend before the influence of the Byzantine political hierarchy. The Pope had to energetically intervene, by the intermediary of the archbishop of Ragusa, and he succeeded in returning the bishops of these regions to his obedience.

The great Empire reconstituted by Manuel Conmène did not last, being closely linked to the extraordinary personality of this great knight in the fashion of the West. But these renewed expeditions against Hungary, through the territories of the Serbian interior, had a great result for the Serbian race and serious consequences for the Albanian nation, embroiled for a long time in all the grandeur and decadence of the Slavs, their neighbors. The Serbia and Adriatic Sea of the kings never returned, but in exchange, in the interior there arose, with an élan that nothing could stop, the New Orthodox Serbia, of Byzantine customs, of the grand-Zupan of Rascia, enemies simultaneously of Byzantium, Hungary and Catholic and maritime Serbia. The new dynasty of Nemanja arrived, from 1074, in the regions of Duklja and Antivari, sidelining Michel II, the son of Bodin, who it saw as merely a count or cnèze. These princes of Eastern rite were the declared adversaries of the Metroplite of Dukjla, the bishop of Salone or Spalato and of the deposed head of the Antivari diocese.

The Pope organized a resistance around the archiepiscopal Seat of Ragusa. This did not prevent the extension of the possessions of the grand-Zupan between the lake of Scutari and the coast of the sea, with the possession of Budua, Antivari and Drivasto. A delegate and relative of the head of the dynasty, Vican, resided on this bank of the Adriatic until the beginning of the 13th century, having at their side an archbishop of Dukjla.

The Holy Seat then had to cede. It only asked for a simple recognition of its authority from the grand-Zupan, without asking it to abandon the Orthodox rite, to grant it this royal title, belonging to the heritage of the old Serbian masters of the sea.

IV
THE ALBANIANS AND THE CRUSADE

This time, the Albanians, having twice escaped the danger of being rendered Grecian, appeared to be fated to disappear in the Slav mass. What saved them was the participation of the Venetians in the new crusade which, in conquering Zara for the Republic in passing, led in 1204 to the establishment of a Latin Empire of Constantinople, of which one the great feudatories was the Doge himself, master of "a quarter and a half" of the Empire.

This "quarter and a half" also contained, according to the agreement of division, all the province of Durazzo, all Albanian territory up to Vagenetia and to Glavanitza, opposite the isle of Corfu. Again, Western influence made its solemn entry into the Balkan peninsula via the door which was Albania.

In its new Balkan province, Venice left unchanged the old administrative divisions, down to the *catepan* which oversaw the castles. In Durazzo, the custom of establishing a duke was kept. We encounter in this situation at the beginning of the thirteenth century, Marino Valaresso. A catepan commanded the local fleet. The Byzantine archbishop had been replaced, naturally, by a Latin prelate, subject to the Latin patriarch of Constantinople. It was not long before he left Albanian territory to function in Venice itself.

This Venetian attempt, which extended as far as Ragusa, was however premature. Venice soon had to abandon the grand role it had envisaged in these regions. But what remained was the Latin religious organization, restored by the triumphant crusade. Ragusa had definitively vanquished Antivari, which had resisted it for so long. Some Latin prelates were resident in Scutari and other points on the peninsula. An *albanensis* bishop, Paul, had an archdeacon as representative in Durazzo.

But already the Greeks had recovered from the light-headedness caused by the great catastrophe of 1204. While fugitives raised the imperial standard in Trebizond and Nicaea, the son of a sebastokrator from Arta, used to living among Albanians and Vlachs, Michaelitzes, who had spent some time in Durazzo and had married a rich heiress from this region, belonging to a Greek family, founded a despotate of Epirus as a continuation of the Byzantine duchy on the Adriatic coast. Michael Comnène, calling himself "lord of Romania", that is Byzantine emperor, was during his turbulent reign the Greek leader of the Albanian race and the suzerain of Vlach autonomy in the mountains.

This provisional state of Epirus could not have a Greek character, since there were no Greek populations with a pro-independence tendency or a military organization with traditions of autonomy. We do not see any mass colonization in these regions in a more recent epoch. The military forces which were employed by the Comnènes to maintain and extend their domination, which it seemed could reach Constantinople itself, could only then belong to the Albanians and Vlachs of the "Greater Walachia" mentioned also in the French sources of the Fourth Crusade and for which towards the start of the fourteenth century Bodonitza formed the natural port on the side of the Archipelago.

Michel Comnène, very solicitous insofar as to the privileges of his subjects, who would not have followed him otherwise, also had to pay attention to the interests and susceptibilities of the Venetians. He confirmed to them the rights accorded by Emperor Manuel and paid a tribute to the Republic, sending as sign of homage, beyond his forty-two pounds per year, a piece of gold, on St Mark's day. He recognized himself as vassal of the Seigniory for his possessions of Vrego, in the duchy of Durazzo, and towards Lepanto. He declared also holding from the Venetian Republic the province of Colonia and the *chartolorat* of Glavanitza. Later, the district of Lepanto was separated from the rest of the Comnène possessions to form a "duchy" in favor of his successors.

This policy was also followed by Michel's successor, Theodore I Comnène (1219-30), who also took the title of Ducas. De facto, his domination extended only to the regions of the North, whereas the South belonged to his brother Constantis. In the East, for the district of Scutari, the Despotate of Epirus had some troubles with the Serb state which, it seems, had to cede.

Under the ecclesiastical relationship, Ochrida remained the hierarchical center but later the coastal districts would attach themselves to the Seat of Naupacte or Lepanto, on which the bishops resident in clearly Albanian territory, in Ianina and Arta, were also dependent. This other archbishopship extended its influence to Larissa, on the one coast, and Durazzo, on the other. Corfu took its direction from Lepanto. We find synods in the town of Arta, under the rule of this Metropolite of the South, in 1223. On one occasion, an ecclesiastical chief appeared in Gardiki, in the regions later subject to the tyranni-

cal authority of Ali Pasha of Janina. Thanks to this ecclesiastical organization, so extensive and so complicated, the two Comnènes,
Michel and Theodore, would merit being awarded the title of de-
fenders of orthodoxy by archbishop Demetrios Chomatianos.

Now, the existence of a national Albania, on a territory inhabited
by this single race, can no longer be doubted. When Jean Asen, Tsar
of the Bulgars, who would put an end to the existence of Epirus,
granted a trading privilege he placed the district of Diavoli in the
"country of the Arbanases". The well-known inscription of Tronovo,
in which the Bulgar sovereign lists all his possessions, also contains a
mention of the "country of the Arbanaes" alongside a "Greek country"; the Bulgaria of Jean Asen extended to Durazzo itself. The synods
of the despot Michel were frequented, according to a contemporary
text, both by "Illyrian and "Bulgar" bishops. Albanian shepherds, in
every way similar to the famous Vlach shepherds, are mentioned mid-
way through the twelfth century.

In 1223, Theodore of Epirus succeeded in taking Salonika, which
had until then belonged to the Latins. Some years later, he resolved
to have himself crowned, and the patriarch of Ochrida performed the
ceremony. This meant breaking peace with an ally, the Bulgar Tsar.
The conflict ended with the catastrophic defeat of Epirus at Cloco-
nitza (1230). Theodore, captured by his victorious adversary, was
later blinded.

Hi dynasty and his state would never recover from this blow, although the blinded Theodore was later restored to his possessions. He
would continue a precarious political existence for some years, as subsequently did the two Manuels, the first of which resided in Salonika.
We see the first of these princes occupy, when the occasion presented

itself, Prilep, Veles, and the "Albanian fortress" (*albanikon*) "of Froia" which has been identified by some with Albanon and which was accorded a privilege in 1253 by the emperor of Nicaea, the master of a great part of the Balkan peninsula; a second privilege was granted for the same fortress in 1255 by Theodore Lascaris, another emperor of Nicaea. In 1256, Nicephore, son of Michel II of Epirus, married Marie, daughter of the Nicaean emperor Theodore and on this occasion, the empire of Nicaea again obtained Albanian possessions, like Serfidsche, and even rights over Durazzo.

But the Albanians preferred to have a prince of their own. That is why they supported Michel II in his attempt to sideline the Asian imperials. So, they saw in this bastard of the Comnènes not only their legitimate sovereign, but the representative, by customs and interests, if not by blood, of their race.

But from 1258 this Greek dynasty opened the road to a new Western, Catholic and Italian domination. Michel married his daughter Helen to the Hohenstaufen Manfred, Prince of Taranto and successor to Emperor Frederick II in the Kingdom of the Two Sicilies, and gave to his son Corfu, Sopoto, Avlona, Canina, Belgrade and Durazzo itself as dowry; a Neapolitan governor was thus established on the Balkan coast of the Adriatic Sea.

There was however another Orthodox competitor to be sidelined before a Latin Albania could be established. At the beginning of the thirteenth century, of the coast of Dulcigno and Antivari, there reigned a son of the Zupan Vican, from the family of Nemanja, who had for a moment borne the royal title. This prince of Duklja had under his orders a certain number of "counts" or cnezes, such as Miroslav of Dulcigno, Paul, son of Leon, of Alessio. Ragusa itself was several times on the point of succumbing, notably in 1252. A duchy of Chelmo or Chelm emerged at the same time, dependent on the ecclesiastical relationship of both Ragusa and Antivari, whose archbishop in 1256 bore the title of "archiepiscopus sclavinensis" or "archbishop of the Serbs". Albanians were undoubtedly found in greater number among the subjects of these Serb princes who appeared to desire the revival of the kingdom of Duklja, previously entirely Catholic and clearly Western.

But already alongside these Albanians belonging to the Serbs and others whose master was a Greek, we find princes of Albanian race who did not recognize any subjection. Namely Progon, who bore for the Greeks the title of "archon" which means "dominus" and for his own part that of "judex" or "judge", analogous to the title borne in the thirteenth and fourteenth centuries by the first chiefs of political organization among the Romanians of the Danube and the Carpathians.

If the foreign masters, Greek, Serb, and Western, had evacuated Albanian territory, just as around the same time the Tatars and Magyars had to abandon the Romanian territory of Wallachia, this "judge of the Albanians" could have been a strain of independent princes. From this time there would have been a free and single Albania, following the same development as the Romanian Land of the thirteenth century. All the same Progon founded a dynasty, leaving two sons, Demetre and Ghin or Gin, and the latter's daughter married one Gregoire Camonas, who was perhaps not Greek, since he was lord of Croya. As for Demetre, he had the signal honor of marrying a Comnène by blood, the daughter of the grand-Zupan Etienne, who had himself married Eudoxie, daughter of the emperor Alexis III.

This showed us the importance that this Albanian political formation had already gained. For, in Walachia also, the importance acquired by the new state was shown by the marriage concluded between Prince Radu and Kallinikia, belonging to the Byzantine imperial family.

The importance of this Albanian lord is also fixed by the titles accorded to him by the contemporary Byzantines: *sebastos, pansebastos*. These same titles were accorded to one Jean Plytos, Albanian himself, who, after having played a role in Ochrida, Croia and Veria, then became one of the dignitaries of Michel of Epirus and a supporter of Camonas, who had enjoyed similar success alongside the Nemanjics.

And in the same era Croya hosted a bishop subject under the political relationship to this lord. It was already a beginning of ecclesiastical organization as such.

The work begun by the Albanian princes was continued by Goulamos, "of the Albanians" who appeared around 1250. Some have traced his name to the Slave word *golem*, "the great," but it could well be that it amounts to a form derived from the Western name of Guillaume.

It should be recalled finally that Albanian names appear at this epoch in relation to specific personalities; a Tanus, a Ghin.

But, to prevent the progress of the Albanian race towards independence, the Neapolitans appeared on the Balkan coast, at the time that the old Theodore, blind, had withdrawn from the coast of Veria and Vodena.

V
THE ALBANIANS AND THE ANGEVINS OF NAPLES

The Hohenstaufen had been replaced in Naples, following the battle of Benevent, which put an end to the domination of this dynasty, who put an end to the domination of this dynasty, by the enterprising lineage of Charles of Anjou. From the beginning, the hardy brother of Saint Louis was bent on seizing the Albanian coast. As prince of Morea, he had claims on Constantinople and he had ensured himself a title of legitimacy by concluding a treaty of cession with the last Latin emperor, Baudouin II, six years after the return of the Palaiologos to the Byzantine throne. By this treaty of Viterbe, the Angevins obtained the transfer of the country from Michel and all that the emperors demanded in the Albanian and Serb regions of the West of the Peninsula (there was an express distinction between "Albania" and "Serbia"). Albania was considered in this deed as a *regnum*, like a very determined country, and in 1272, Charles of Anjou negotiated with the nobles of these regions for the recognition of himself and his son as "King of Albania" (*reges Albanie*). The second representative of these "kings", Jean de Noytel, was sent, according to the deed itself, "to take possession of the kingdom of Albania" (*ad recipiendum regnum Albanie*).

The Neapolitan troops would occupy Corfu and Avlona. In 1272, Durazzo, included in the royal province, obtained a privilege, and Charles accorded it a vicar, a "captain of the Albanians", ca*pitanus*

Albanarum, belonging to the Albanian nation itself. This same year the viceroy of Albania, the "marshal", was Guillaume Bernard, of French nationality.

It was in vain that the Paleologus of Constantinople sought to win back the heritage of the despots of Epirus. The moral support accorded by the Orthodox patriarch of Ochrida did not help them fulfil this goal.

For the Albanian nobility, which the Angevin registers of Naples so often mention, was, according to the Latin traditions of the country, sincerely attached to the principles of the Crusade. Those who failed in their undertakings were imprisoned in the royal castles.

Some of these chieftains bore the title of *cneze*, which means judge; like a *comes Albanie*; others conserved the Byzantine characterization of sebastos,; on one occasion we also encounter the Slave title of Zupan. As to the name of these princes, they often belong to the local or national tradition; Gropa, Paul, Zacharie, Sguro, Tanus, Topia, Mile, Alexis, Arianites (a family of the Zaccarias plays a role in Albania in the early fifteenth century, such as Croya Zaccaria). The Western influence meant that some of them were entitled "barons" like nobles of the Kingdom of Naples. Naturally, the information we have on these personalities is not enough to establish their real role in the region, but what we have is sufficient to note that a nation was emerging on the political horizon.

This Neapolitan expansion formed part of the great French national expansion in the Middle Ages, which, by passing through Naples, was directed towards this East where the same French had created, from the beginning of the twelfth century, these crusade states. After Charles I and Charles II the Lame, Albania had a French master of its own in the form of Prince Phillip of Taranto.

The representatives of the Angevin kings and princes did not, of course, enjoy a domination exempt from dangers and intrigues. We also see the "captain of Romania" (*capitaneus Romanie*) which means the royal representative for the Byzantine empire, fighting for the old residence of the kings of Croatia, the castle of Belgrade or Biogradee (*castrum Beligradi*). Some Saracens, descendants of the Muslim colonists established by Frederick II in Lucera, like Musa, captain of the Saracens, fought under the Latin flags. But the main actors in these conflicts were the Albanians themselves, and among *them we find the first representative of this family of the Mussachi (Johannes* dictus Mussaei) who was, in fact Vlach in origin (Mussachi-Musat). Jean Musacchi, who fought the Neapolitans, was taken to Avlona and imprisoned in the castle of Brindisi. In a combat against the Paleologus of Constantinople under the walls of Belgrade, we can distinguish the Albanian Matiga or Mangiaista, and among his contemporaries we find a count of Albania (*comes de Albania*), Maurus or Maurice. Durazzo sent a special contingent, the *homines Duracchii et Albanie*.

The king himself stated that "the taking of the castle of Belgrade was dearer to his heart than he can say." But this little war, which continued until 1281, was not favorable to the Latins; their "marshal of Romania," one Sully, known as Russo, was seized, and no successor was sent. The *regnum Albaniae* would not then belong in a full and durable manner to the king of Naples.

But the Greeks of Constantinople were no longer capable of seizing this "kingdom" and, as for the rest of the Despotate of Epirus, the successors of Conmène were not able to claim a similar heritage. The son of the despot Nicephore and Anne, a very enterprising and ambitious princess, Thomas, only disposed of a very narrow territory in Epirus properly so called. The Principality of Lepanto had an absolutely separate existence. Jean Ducas, who administered it, was the suzerain of Thessalonian Greater Walachia. It was in vain that the emperor of Byzantium, supported by the chief of the Catalan adventurers established on Empire land, tried to subject this Vlach Thessaly, replacing the despot Jean by his own son, Theodore. If in fact Jean was fixed on an appanage of old age on the coast of Aetolia this coastal part of the former Despotate remained autonomous until the beginning of the fourteenth century, just as until 1318 the domination of the said Thomas was maintained in Epirus properly so called. And this Epirus increasingly became exclusively Albanian, by opposition to the Grace of Constantinople also, whereas the coastal part, Thessalonian and Aetolian, became increasingly Romanian Vlach.

We have already spoken of the campaigns undertaken by the Paleologus against Epirus; the Byzantine Caesars naturally felt the need to reform the Empire in its old extension. "The son of schismatic Paleologus, our enemy" — such was the characterization given to him by the Neapolitans — had at its disposal a powerful army, composed in part of foot soldiers, of great use against the French cavalry. For a while there were fears for the possession of Durazzo and Avlona, above all for the latter, whose loss would have been particularly dangerous for the interests of the king. However, the long dynastic discord between Andronic the elder and Andronic the younger meant that his war, undertaken under such happy auspices, was interrupted and Neapolitan domination saved for some further time.

Such was the situation in the fourteenth century, when a new Greek offensive, coming from Constantinople, was directed against Vlach Thessaly, occupying the well-known Romanian center of Metzovo. As the Paleologus were allied to the Genoese, with whose

aid they had succeeded in conquering Constantinople itself, a Genoese fleet appeared at the same time in the Ambracian gulf. The despot
of Epirus resorted to the support of the Latin feudatories who occupied Achaea. No combat took places, as the Byzantine troops, seized
by panic, fled before Janina.

There had been a question at a given moment of a marriage between the daughter of the despot Nicephore, Tama, and the heir of
the Empire. This alliance did not take place, but, in exchange, Marie,
sister of Tamar, married count Richard of Cephalonia, one of the
Neapolitan barons; the marriage had as dowry the island of Lefkada.
The political situation of the despot had been visibly strengthened.

At this time the main role in the "kingdom of Albania" was played,
alongside the Latins, by Philip of Taranto, already mentioned. As
Thomas was killed by his nephew, count Nicolas of Cephalonia
(1318-23) in 1318, Neapolitan influence soon had no rival capable
of blocking its progress. Philip obtained, as has already been said, the
transfer of all his rights from the dispossessed emperor of Constantinople, and he henceforth posed himself as the heir of the Catholic
Caesars of Byzantine. In 1292 Catherine, titular empress of Constantinople, ceded to him Achaea and the city of Athens, "the kingdom
of Albania and the province of Walachia." This ambitious career was
supported also by the marriage concluded in 1393 between this
prince and Tamar, the daughter, already mentioned, of the despot
Nicephore.

VI
ALBANIAN EXPANSION
AT THE END OF THE MIDDLE AGES

During these events, princes and lords of Albania appeared several times among the combatants; around 1280 a Guillaume of Albania fell to the power of the Latins; other "Albanenses" met the same fate. In the service of the King of Naples, we find one Pierre of Avlona, bearing the Greek title of *sebastos*. The *nobiliores Albaniae* are mentioned more than once. King Charles gave forgiveness to a Georges or Calgeorges Sgouro or "Scura." There is even a reference to a sebastos resident in Spinarezza.

The Albanians appear around 1300 also in regions which had not previously belonged to them and where they did not have a mass implantation. We thus see them near Ragusa, overlooked by mountains where Romanian Vlachs lived as cheese traders and caravan drivers, the "mountain Vlachi" often mentioned in the accounts of the little Republic, with the noting of their "caseus valachicus." Towards the beginning of the foourteenth century, a note in the sources shows that the Albanian language was employed in the same elevated regions (*in monta in lingua albanesca*). Albanians were also found at the head of the caravans which penetrated into Serbia, like "Marc Alvanes" and "Todor Arbanese."

The names borne by these Albanians are in part traditional names and in part others, borrowed from the Slavs; the son of one Miroslav is thus called Jean, or Ghin. We see in the documents names like Gianni, Vita, Manega. Once an Albanian bears the Roman name of Negru; "Ella Negro, Albanese."

Often these Albanians were colonized on the lands of nobles and convents, like their neighbors, the Romanian shepherds.

The value of the lands in Serbia grew. Sometimes they would be used to herd cattle "according to the custom of the land" (*secundum usum terrae*); sometimes these colonists became farmers.

The Albanian upper class at this time bore pompous titles, like that of *sebastos* and of great *hétairiarque*. Alongside the apprentices who entered in the workshops of the industrialist of the different towns of the costs — where Gin Mylbraich sent his son Medoe to learn a trade with Bogoe Palilogo, artisan of Cattaro, and Marcull, daughter of the Albanian Marc, once a hostess by trade (*posaica*) in the service of Jean Basilii, entrusted her son to the goldsmith Medoss Drongovitsch — we find rich individuals, like Progon, son of Sguro, who appear among the donors to churches — in this special case of Saint Clement in Ochrida.

Avlona formed an independent republic, whose inhabitants devoted themselves to piracy. Although Andronic Paleologus, son of Assanes, appeared as the master of the coast of Avlona, Belgrade and Spinarizza, to pass then to Ianina, the "republican" character of Avlona was maintained. Among those who enriched themselves as corsairs we find in 1312 one Demetre Ganza. Venice had to defend itself against these hardy disturbances to the security of the seas.

This development of the Albanian race was once more hindered by a movement from the interior. Orthodox Serbia, whose chieftain bore the title of king, again expanded towards the coast of the Adriatic Sea. It found an agent of expansion in the exceptional personality of Queen Helene, originally from the West — a French woman. She founded several places of pilgrimage, like the convent of Saint Mark in Scutari, that of Saint Mark in Dulcigno, the houses of St François in Cattaro and in Antivari. Her sister, Marie, married to the Frenchman Anselme of Chaurs, functioned as a sort of queen in Dukjla, whose name was henceforth replaced by that of the river of Zenta. The two sisters were founders of the monastery of Saint Mark at Rotac. They worked actively to destroy the heresy of the Patarenes in neighboring Bosnia, and they sought to attract to the Catholic religion the new chieftain of the Bulgars, Georges Terteri, a Cuman from the coast of Vidin.

The two princesses represented in Dulcigno, Antivari, Ragusa, Cattaro, Scutari, and in the Zenta a new Western influence, which returned in another form at a time when the strength of the Neapolitans began to wane.

This influence had nothing to do with that of Venice, which was older. The republic of Saint Mark, in continual conflict with the pirates of Avlona, presented demands in 1320 against the despot of Epirus himself, who the emperor of Constantinople defended as being his vassal. The Venetians' rivals, the Genoese, also appeared in these waters that had hitherto been foreign to them.

Again, we see, around 1340, a Serb offensive, on the coast of Macedonia as well as that of Thessaly. This offensive was led by the greatest sovereign of the Serbs in the Middle Ages, Etienne Douchane, who desired and obtained, thanks to the conflict between the young Paleologos of Constantinople and his tutor, Jean Cantacuzène, the title of Tsar, emperor of the Serbs and the Greeks — and the Albanians also. It was in vain that King Robert of Naples, the successor of Charles II, tried to counterbalance this hegemony by inciting the Albanians against the Serb sovereign, as he did in 1330. We see the Neapolitan Prince Louis concluding a treaty with André Mussachi, to whom Constantinople had awarded the title of despot; a privilege was accorded to Tanus Topia, master of the territory near Durazzo, and in Durazzo itself another Neapolitan prince, Charles, functioned in the capacity of duke (1319-23).

But already in 1343 Douchane set a garrison in Croia; the "imperator Stephanus" exerted an influence as suzerain over the town of Cattaro.

Although already his predecessor Ouroch bore with pride the title of dominator "of the sea until the river of the great Danube" (*a mari usque ad flumen Dannubil magni*), the Slav emperor founded his state above all on the possession of Macedonia; it tended towards Salonika, which means it was fatally detached from this Adriatic coast, which however was such an important part of his states. Serb domination would then only be in these regions a preparation for that of the republic of Venice, of which Stephen himself had become the citizen.

The Neapolitans kept in their former province, once a kingdom, only Durazzo, where the Topia exercised nearly unlimited rights, and the Ionian isles, over which the power of the palatine counts of Cephalonia, who also had links in Epirus, extended.

VII
ALBANIAN STATES

Now Avlona, like the neighboring castle of Canina, was a seigniory, having at its head the brother of the Bulgar wife of Stephen Dušan. This lord took at the same time the title of Conmène and of Asen.

If there is a question here of a doubtful Conmène, a Cantacuzène invaded Thessaly, the same person who disputed Jean Paleologus's claim to the Byzantine throne. He was able to ensure the possession of this Vlach Thessaly for one of his sons.

Finally, in Epirus the influence of the counts of Cephalonia led to the domination of an Italian of the House of Oraini, Nicolas (1318-23) who had however gone over to the Greek religion. The Toccos, also Neapolitans, would soon replace the Oraini in these possessions. As for the new Greek despot of Epirus, Nicephore, he was vanquished by Jean Cantacuzène and his allies, the Albanians. Deported from Salonika to the Dardanelles, he sought refuge in Thessaly and Acarnania, where the troops of Douchane's successor, Simeon Ouroch, repelled him. He resorted to the support of the Turks, but despite this crime against his religion and race, he lost the battle near the river Achelous in 1358, and thus ended his days.

In the second half of the fourteenth century, the Serbs were everywhere the masters. Simeon Ouroch, already mentioned, was in Thessaly and he appears among the donors of the famous convents

of Meteora; the prince of Greater Walachia, Jean Ducas, had trans-
ferred the land to him. Jean, son of Simeon, was sidelined in the despotate of Epirus by his brother in law Thomas Prelioubovitsch.

But the great mass of the population in this Epirus remained Albanian, and the Albanians and Vlachs also formed the majority of the
population of the coast of Lepanto, where Neapolitan domination
still vegetated, and in Avlona, where Jean Comnène Asen continued
to reign until 1363.

To break this Serbian domination the Ottoman invasion was necessary, with all that which it contributed as advantages and disad-
vantages for the Albanian race.

At the time when the first Ottoman bands appeared in the valleys
of the Pindus, the Albanians, mixed here and there with the Vlachs,
formed the very basis of the populations and had a notable participation in its affairs, as much in Thessaly, where prince Jean, soon to
become the monk Joseph, employed Greek in his chancellery, as in
the Epirote possessions of the Serb Prelioubovitsch, whose widow
Marie, daughter of Simeon Ourouch, bore the dynastic title of the
Ange, Ducas and Paleologus, residing at Janina, and finally in the
province of Arta, now detached from the principality of Leponto,
which however kept the archiepiscopal seat. In this town of Arta, the
Albanians were governed by a lord of their race. He belonged to the
line of the Boua Spata, which kept power for a long time.

A Florentine, Esau of the Buondelmonti, would later receive the
heritage of these aboriginal lords.

A Greek chronicle from Janina presents us with what happened in
Epirus during the years following the imperial domination of Dušan

and his brother and the collapse of the Greek domination of the despots.

In 1358 Nicephore Ducas, brother of the empress Anne and the last of these Byzantine masters of the province, was killed — as we have said — in combat against the Albanians, among whom new tribes had risen to a preponderant situation, often with the Vlach element dominant, the Bous, the Malakassi, the Massaraki, of whom the first two above all can be considered as belonging to the Romanian nationality.

If the Serb Caesar Simeon Ouroch, who set up his wife in Tricala, occupied Arta and Janina, despite the opposition of Hlapen, he abandoned Aetolia to the mountaineers.

A little later, the succession of this latter Slav "emperor" was taken by the son, who had joined his mother at Vodena in Macedonia, of Prelioub and his Serb wife, Thomas, who had in 1367 married the "Paleologos", Marie Angeline. He was a cruel tyrant of inexorable severity, with a true passion for torture and murder — a precursor of the terrible Ali Pasha.

He was incited to his acts of vengeance by the continued attempts of the Albanian chieftains who, after establishing themselves in other towns of Epirus, hoped to be able to do the same in Janina itself. One such was Pierre Liocha, a Romanian by origin, who obtained in marriage for his son Ghin, as the price of peace, Irene, daughter of Thomas. Pierre occupied Arta from 1360 to 1374. From 1304 a new line of Spatas appeared amidst the tribe of Boua, of which it even bore the name, likened perhaps to the old Arianites, the contemporary of Scanderbeg. They dominated in Argyrokastron, near the coast, and in the port of Lepanto, soon coveted by Venice as well as by the

Turks. After the death of Pierre Liocha, Jean or Ghin Boua Spatas
united under the same regime the two Albanian centers of Epirus; he
also had the honor of an alliance with the House of Prelioub, by marrying Helene, sister of the despot whose capital he had hoped to occupy. It was in vain that the Grand Master of the Order of Saint John,
who had possessions in Greece, Jean Fernandez de Heredia, tried to
sideline him; the valiant Spanish knight was taken in combat in 1377
and had to be ransomed. Around the same time Janina was also
threatened by another bandit chieftain, Ghin known as *Frate*
("brother" in Romanian) which certainly does not mean a defrocked
Latin monk, who these Albanians and Romanians of Eastern rite
would not have accepted as chief. We should also note another competitor for domination of Epirus who wanted to seize it after the
death of Thomas, killed by his own henchmen, Bougoes (in Romanian "Vagaiu") who the chronical cited characterizes disdainfully,
showing the bizarre national character of this adventurer, Serb-Alba-
nian-Bulgar and Vlach. Ghin Zenebissi, an authentic Albanian, was
also present to dispute a province remaining without a master.

But Janina would not belong to them. At the death of Thomas
son of Prelioub, in 1403, his widow joined his brother, the monk
Joseph, and together they installed as new despot the brother of the
duchess of Leucade, Esau of Buondelmonti, who had married the
daughter of Ghin Spatas. He had the mission of defending Epirus
against the Turks, whose vanguards had appeared in these regions
under a certain Chahim from 1380-1390. As for Ghin himself, for
whom the Greek chronicle abounds in elegies, he died in 1400, leaving Arta to his brother Sgouros. Some years later, the flag of Saint
Mark was lifted over the citadel of Lepanto.

Some Albanian lords were also found around 1370 in Castoria, the residence of Hlapen, whose daughter Helene married the Serb hero, of rather reduced historic proportions, Marc Cralievitsch. Bertho also formed part of the possessions of this parvenu. In Ochrida itself, the veritable ecclesiastical capital of western, Macedonian "Bulgaria", the master was now the Albanian Andre Gropa. Hlapen, already mentioned, had married the mother of Thomas Prelioubovitsch. Hlapen's son, Stephen, also took the title of Ducas, at a time when the last representatives of Christian domination in Thessaly, the Philantropenos, called themselves both "Angeli" and "Caesars of Walachia."

Durazzo belonged for many years to the Albanian Charles Topia, despite the attempts at recuperation by the Neapolitans, who employed the services of a Frenchman, Enguerrand de Coucy, and others. He recognized the rights of suzerainty of the Neapolitan duchess of Durazzo, Jeanne, married successively to Louis d'Evreux and to Robert d'Artois.

Avlona found new masters in the decadent Conmènes, whose domination ended with Princess Roughina, Albanian in name. But if the Albanian character of this seigneury is incontestable, we must admit this also for most of the more extensive and ambitious principality of the Zenta, at the head of which appeared, after 1360, members of the Balcha family, doubtless of Romanian origin; in 1385, Balcha, son of Balcha, bore the title of duke of Durazzo.

This dynasty, which lasted until nearly halfway through the fifteenth century, extended both to the coast of Cattaro and that of Prizrend and Trebigne. Balcha, already mentioned, was for some time the husband of the Conmène of Avlona. He also possessed Antivari and Alessio. Legend attributes to him familial relations with the Albanian princes, of whom the Doucachines, Leca and Paul, remained masters of Alessio, while the Ionimas held lands around Durazzo.

Balcha accepted the difficult mission of defending the Albanian territories against the Turkish invasion. He fell in battle in September 1385, near to the course of the Voioussa, on the territory of the Massachi. After him Thopia continued to bear the title of "lord of Albania." Alessio and Budua remained in the hands of the princes of this race. Antivari and Dulcigno, as well as the neighboring castle of Dagno, remained the apanage of the Balchides.

But all these little lords could only count on their own, much reduced, forces, and their weak treasuries were hardly enough to stop the Ottoman conquest. Before the death of Topia, Durazzo was offered to the republic of Venice, who dealt with it seriously, while hoping to keep good neighborly relations with Sultan Murad and his Turks whose Seigneury suspected little of the great future. Measures were taken for the defense of this this gateway to Albania. Roughina of Avlona was considered as having particular sympathies for the Venetians, already masters of Corfu, bought from the Neapolitans, and disposing of increasingly numerous territories in the Peloponnese. Venice viewed with concern the establishment of a Turkish officer, Baiezid, in the mountains of Albania and the influence he gained daily over the holders of the neighboring castles. Thus, Durazzo was occupied, in 1392. A bailiff and a captain were established there, as well as a rector and an admiral. There were negotiations with the Doucachines and the Serb Raditsch Tschrnoievitsch, baron of the regions of the Zenta, for the possession of Alessio, "the right eye of Durazzo". The annexation of Croia, where the Venetian Marc Barbadigo was established, but as a vassal of the Turks, was considered.

Only the Balchides, Georges Strachimir and the third Balcha resisted, defending to the end the heritage of their family against Venetian avidity. Long battles, which can be followed virtually day by day, were needed against the Albanian coalition formed around these increasingly de-nationalized Slavs to arrive at the definitive establishment of the Venetians in Bude, Dulcigno, Dagno and Antivari, where already before the end of the fourteenth century the Turks had begun to penetrate. The two Doucachines, Tanus and Progon, son of Leca, had abandoned Alessio to the Republic. As for Croya, it had belonged to another member of the Balcha dynasty, Constantin, who also disposed of Dagno with its customs houses; finally, he was killed in fighting against the Venetians. Constantin's heir, Nicetas Topia, had always held cordial relations with the Republic. To meet its goals, Venice also had to fight of the claims of the neighboring Serb lords, Sandali, of Bosnia, who had married Helene, widow of Balcha III, and Hrvoie.

The last of the Balchas ended his days in April 1421. His heritage was claimed also by the new chief of Serbia, George Brancovich, whose troops, fighting against Venice, would occupy Drivasto, Antivari and Budua. Venice did not however abandon its claims, which rested on long sacrifices of money and hard-won victories. To conserve its Albanian possessions, against Brancovich as well as against the pretender Stephen of Maramonte, the Republic agree to pay a tribute to the Turks.

VIII
SCANDERBEG

The last and most knowledgeable historian of the Serbs, Jirecek, recognized that in the armies of Tsar Dušan, above all in those he employed for the lower regions of his domination, the soldiers belonged to the Albanian race. We can even go further to completely
fix the part played by Albanians in the foundation and maintenance
of this last Slav counterfeit of the Byzantine Empire. This Empire
represented Roman centralization, strengthened again by the political influence of the Orient: an adored sovereign, a glittering Court,
a complicated organization of ranks and functions, a capital.
Whereas the Serb state of the fourteenth century, as it resulted from
the conquests of the "emperor", had only a military chief, barely
surrounded by a few dignitaries, without a fixed capital and retain-
ing under its hegemony rather than under its orders local lords who
were very much the masters of their own territory. It was a true
Balkan feudality. And if we wish to admit the influence of the Angevin regime, this influence itself was exerted solely on the Albanian element and was thus transmitted to the new foundation by
the sole intermediary of his people.

Participating in the expeditions of Dušan, who desired possession,
along with Macedonia as a whole, of Salonika, the natural capital of
the province, the Albanians were naturally directed towards the
South, and many of them, following the current, already old — as we
have seen — towards agriculture, did not return to their valleys,

continually exposed to the attacks and looting of the Turks. One of the combatants for the Byzantine crown during the second half of the fourteenth century, Manuel Cantacuzene, used to employ Albanians, at a time when one could hardly ignore the competition of the Turks on every front, sending numerous mercenaries from the Pindus into the Morea itself, whereas others, like the "*Compagnie des aventuriers Catalans*" [Company of Catalan Adventurers] , established Albanian camps which remained, in continental Greece.

Venice, as soon as it had Corfu and the coastal towns, hastened to send soldiers of this nation to all its colonies, old and new, beyond the Adriatic.

It should also be admitted that one of the reasons for which this migration continued in the fifteenth century was the conquest by the Turks of the regions of coastal Albania, defended, not without courage, by the Tocco, of Neapolitan origin. Janina was occupied in 1430, Arta nineteen years later. The Tocco conserved only Cephalonia, the cradle of their power, and Zante.

The Republic's relations with the lords of the interior, which it would have liked to have as condottieri in its service, extended until Emathia, in the purely Albanian country of Mat. Ivan Castriota, who called himself thus, although he was of pure Shqiptar race, with a Serb first name and a Greek surname — *kastrioiis* means bourgeois, the inhabitant of a fortified town — thus had accidental political relations with the Venetians, although he was forced to adopt the suzerainty of the Turks. He had to give them as hostage, according to custom, one of his sons, born of a Slav wife — another of the children bore the Serb name of Stanicha, a third that of Repoch — George and, as opportunities were not lacking at the Court of the Sultan,

where an intelligent representative of the conquered races could rise
to the most brilliant and remunerative situations, Georges Castriota
became the "prince Alexander" of the Turks, Scanderbeg.

This happened at a time when one could hardly suspect the ap-
proach of a great movement of Christian recuperation, a new crusade
destined to a deliver and strengthen Byzantium, already ready to succumb. John Hunyadi, a Romanian from Transylvania, who had
passed in the ranks of the dominant caste of the Magyars and had
adopted the Catholic rite, put himself at the head of the armies which
would return the European east to its old masters.

Albania now received that impulsion which put it in a fighting
mood, by designating a goal worthy of its efforts, this Hungary
which, in concert with the Romanians of Wallachia and Moldova
and with the Serbs of the despot Georges Brancovich, who would
soon however prove an unreliable ally, took up the traditions of the
Angevin kings of Naples, the projects of a Charles of Anjou and a
Philip of Taranto.

The first who put faith in the promises of Hunyadi and accepted
his leadership were the Moussachi, the Doucachines, the Topia and
this Arianites Comnène, whose relations with the Greeks — although
his daughter, Angelina, would marry the son of Brancovich — resem-
bled the relations of the Castriotas with the Slavs. It was only two
years later, in 1443, that Scanderbeg returned to his old faith and to
his familial links, beginning a long war, magnified by the generous
legend which forms the eternal glory of his name.

Scanderbeg or Skanderbeg — it is the name under which he was
known to contemporaries as well as posterity — still kept something

of his education amidst the Turks. Fighting cruel enemies, he employed their own means, as would, around twenty years later, the Vlach prince Vlad the Impaler. He did not hesitate, when he captured a rebel nephew, to decapitate him, on a Venetian galley, by his own hand. With a perfect knowledge of the Turkish system of waging war, he benefited from it to stay resolute in circumstances where another would have lost and would soon have paid with his head for the temerity of rebelling against his suzerain and master. But, remaining Albanian in the cores of his being, he liked combat for combat's sake and, devoid of political orientation — because the Turks made him their constant enemy only by their obstinate resolution of seizing Croya, the capital of Scanderbeg, the area of the Albanian vulture, who carried the eagle in his arms — he was, according to the circumstances, for and against Venice, from which he claimed Dagno and Drivasto in 1447 — Venice itself put a price on the head of this enemy — and when, at a certain moment, the Sultan's troops came to repel him, he felt no humiliation in going to continue in Italy, as a simple chief of mercenaries, the cause of this king of Naples who had also been one of his constant protectors.

Barletius, a writer in the style of the Renaissance, and a great lover of tales which were much more interesting than they were authentic, a hardy creator of historic incidents alien to history, has left us what is a poem rather than a biography of the Albanian hero, who was known henceforth on the testimony of this suspect witness. Nothing in the Venetian sources, documents and chronicles, which never lose view of this sometimes threatening neighbor, always worthy of interest, authorizes us to admit the tales of this panegyrist of rich imagination which were very well used in long lost popular songs. What emerges from these sporadic notes, while being much simpler, is not lacking in grandeur, because he had to withstand renewed assaults for twenty years as well as expeditions led by the Sultan himself, Murad II, and his son, Mehmed, the Conqueror of Constantinople, in 1450, then in 1466.

Venice had ended its struggle for the possession of the Zenta against the Serb despot, who even at a time of despair sought a haven on the possessions of the Republic. Blocked in the first phase of its expansion, it no longer pursued, for fear of drawing Turkish vengeance, the old project of annexing the whole of the Albanian lands up to the mountains of the interior. It had to consider the war of the lord of Croya as an action of defense of his own Balkan territory. Aid was not lacking from this side and we can certainly say that without the presence of Venice in the Zenta the second epoch of Skanderbeg's career would have been decidedly impossible. Supporting this chivalrous neighbor, who exerted a mysterious prestige on enemies as well as his own side, was forcing the Turks into a defensive war — without looking like it.

Venice learned with satisfaction of the advance of Scanderbeg on Berat, his attack against the Turks of Dibra and other neighboring castles. These were in part foreigners, but in part also former Christian lords, relatives or traditional rivals of the avenger of the Christians, who had themselves adopted Islam or had inherited it from their brothers. The hatred was only more vivid: revenge, the Albanian vendetta, always famous, had, in these conflicts, at least the role of politics in a higher sense of the word. Such was the case with Mousa, who was in command there, in Dibra. Among the members of the family of the Zenebissi there was also a Turk, Hamza-beg. This recalled the time when the Albanian nobility was divided between the partisans and adversaries of the Neapolitan regime.

But, when the victor of these mountain duels reached the coast of Sainte Marie de Rotac and took under mount Tomor the important castle of Tomornitza, the Sultan decided to wage a war of against him, employing his own legions rather than the Muslim Albanian bands. Then, however, Skanderbeg had the new and precious support of the king of Naples, Alphonse d'Aragon, who, as master also of the Spanish coast, dreamed of an imperial domination extending over the eastern and western basins of the Mediterranean.

This was no longer simply a protector who sent soldiers and money, as had been the case for Venice; the heir of Charles of Anjou wanted to be more than a patron: the valiant Albanian thus become also his vassal according to western practices; we can see this from 1457 by the privilege accorded to him as master of the fortress, of *his* fortress, of Croya. It was a genuine attempt at Neapolitan restoration, in the Angevin style, on the eastern bank of the Adriatic. Scanderbeg was no more than a "captain" of this magnificent and demanding suzerain, just as another ambitious and pompous sovereign, who also claimed to represent the single cause of Christianity, Matthias, King of Hungary, saw as only a vassal, a "captain" of *his* armies in the contemporary Moldavian hero, more powerful and glorious than Scanderbeg, Stephen the Great.

And, just as, at the most difficult time of his resistance, Stephen was abandoned by those who boasted of their support for him, Scanderbeg did not find in the king of Naples a powerful enough support to allow him to resist until the end.

The Moldavian sought refuge in his own more extended country, but Scanderbeg went to Italy to command the Neapolitan troops of one Robert Orsini (1461).

He returned (1462), also leading a Venetian contingent because, at this time, despite its cautious policy, the Republic had been forced to launch a formal war against the Turks. Albania owed its salvation to it, once again.

Soon after there came, in 1466, the supreme effort by Sultan Mehmed. He passed by Bitolia, one of the new centers of Macedonia, and besieged Croya itself. And as, this time one more, the powerful castle, which by its invincible resistance took on a symbolic character, maintaining itself under the flag of Albanian freedom, the conqueror of Constantinople adopted the same measure that his ancestor Mohammed 1st had adopted, in the absence of any better alternative, in relation to Wallachia. He fortified Valona, where the Turks had installed themselves at the beginning of the fifteenth century, and founded in the very midst of this obstinate Christian Albania the great town of Elbassan. Muslim colonies were established while 3,000 Albanian prisoners accompanied the Sultan in his return, fallen from his expectations. A certain Balabanbeg had custody of these regions, — again a native who had embraced Islam.

Again, Scanderbeg had to leave his county, but only to return even more embittered against this rival that he despised. Combats took place near Durazzo, where Venice thought it prudent to send a fleet. As the Sultan had left to foment intrigues among the country's chieftains — as he had done, not without success, in Wallachia, with his "minion" Radu the Handsome, against the brother of this pretender,

Vlad the Impaler — a nephew of the Albanian hero, the latter subjecting him to the torture mentioned above.

But already the forces were also exhausted of he who had for at least twenty years performed a daily miracle of resistance as a minor lord, poor and without close allies or sincere friends, against all the strength of a great Empire, led by a renowned warrior. Before reaching the age of sixty he withdrew, despairing of ever being able to return to his valleys often watered by the blood of his race, to Alessio, among his neighbors, the Venetians, who welcomed him without providing him with new aid. It was there that he died in 1468, this greatest representative of his race, which has never forgotten him.

Venice occupied Croia in 1469, but lost Scutari in 1478. Scanderbeg's widow, Donika, daughter of Arianites Conmène, sought refuge with her son on foreign land, and what had been for a moment a single and same Albania under a flag of victory was quickly divided between the masters of the old districts, the Mussacbi, the Sgouro and so on. Slavs, or Slavified Albanians, like Ivan, son of the condottiere Etienne, in the service of Venice, and husband of an Arianites, in Zabliak, emerged in the most inaccessible regions to attempt the policy which had not succeeded until the end of this extraordinary warrior. Ivan, who also became one of the heroes of legend, founded a Slav-Albanian principality, Montenegro. The Albanian Hoti were among his followers.

IX
AFTER SCANDERBEG:
SUFFERING AND REVOLTS

Scanderbeg's son, don Giovanni, emigrated to Italy, where he obtained fairly extensive possessions from the kings of Naples. One Ferrante, belonging to the same family, is also found among the Neapolitan nobles. We should also mention the descendants, whose series continues until today, of Skanderbeg's elder brother, Stanicha, who became the marquises of Atripalda.

Jirecek also cites the Italianized descendants of the Arianites and Doucachines, who established themselves in Venice and Ancona.

This Moussachi, Andre, who put together in a pamphlet the genealogy of his family, had also suffered the de-nationalizing influence of Italian civilization. With the chieftains, a whole Albanian population left its country of origin to find refuge on the opposite bank of the Adriatic Sea: they are among the most distant ancestors of the Albanians who still today inhabit certain villages of Sicily and whose role in the new cultural life of the nation we will soon see.

But most Albanians henceforth played a role in the invading Ottoman life, whose chieftains did not belong and could not belong to the Turkish race itself, and were thus not very capable of fulfilling political functions. Along with Bulgar and Serb renegades — in very great number —and Greeks, among them some of the highest dignitaries of the Empire in the fifteenth century — we encounter, in an incessantly growing proportion, not only the descendants of the old clan princes, former counts and *cnezes* of the Adriatic coast and the mountains of the interior, but also Shqiptars of low origin.

Some among them were true devotees of Islam, others maintained sympathies for the Christian religion which they had *only formally abandoned*, to meet the needs of their careers: we find crypto-Catholics until the mid-nineteenth century, an era at which they were subject to barbarous persecutions, being deported to Asia Minor, where many of them would succumb to poverty and deprivation. We see this phenomenon of dual religious practice also in Persia, at the beginning of the Muslim domination, when some Iranians obstinately remained secretly adherents of the old faith.

But it was not necessary to embrace the Muslim religion to be able to satisfy the ancestral instinct of warriors. Beyond this new Montenegrin Diocletian, under whose standards, bearing the same Byzantine eagles, war could be continued in the manner of Skanderbeg, perspectives opened in Italy, during wars which would change the face of the peninsula, for all those who wished to make the traditional bravery of the Albanians a skilled trade. A whole book could be written on the Balkan "stradioti" in the service of the different princes and Italian republics of the fifteenth and sixteenth centuries, and among these a good number were of Albanian origin, such as a Boua, Mercurio. The Venetians would often employ them during their wars against the Turks for the possession, not only of Albania — they would lose Durazzo only in 1501 — but also, of the Morea, where these mercenaries could meet other elements, already established in the country, of the same race.

In losing Durazzo, Venice could however conserve its ports, which it had acquired through the payment of money at the end of the four-teenth or beginning of the fifteenth century: Dulcigno, Antivari and Budua. A new, unfortunate war led — despite the great Christian victory at Lepanto— to the first of two of these ports being aban-doned to the Sultan. Chimaira and Sopoto did not remain in the hands of the dethroned Venetians either. Budua alone was conserved on the Albanian coast as an isolated dependency of a Dalmatia which remained Venetian. We know that, among the neighboring islands, Corfu stayed in the possession of the Seigneury until the end of the eighteenth century.

But if the western domination of the Republic of Venice, pulver-ized in this series of lost wars, disappeared almost entirely, the same cannot be said of this other Western influence which was that of the Catholic church. If in the region of the South, in relations with Arta and Ianina, or, during the last time of independence, the Greek ele-ment had dominated in political and religious life, the Albanians re-maining attached to Orthodoxy, the Catholic rite kept its adherents in all the regions of the North and center, where the activity of the missionaries never ceased. They also allowed the use of the national language, even in the ceremonies of the Church, and some time be-fore the German pilgrim Arnold von Harff, coming from Cologne, collected a couple of dozen Albanian words (1496), we encounter, in another Western source, the Albanian formula for baptism, which could be pronounced by the parents of a dying child in the absence of a priest (*Notes et extraits pour servir à l'Histoire des croisades*, V, p. 295.). The oldest books in Albanian, the catechisms, are owed to these representatives of the Catholic religion.

These Latin bishops and their clergy lived in a situation of poverty and complete humility. The religious leaders of the Albanian Catholics did not even have permission to reside in the towns which had been the seat of their predecessors, and these towns offered only miserable ruins, as was the case for Drivasto, Alessio, or Croia, where Christians were not admitted at night until recent times, and for Durazzo itself. Many villages had also been destroyed, and the population, which, from the end of the thirteenth to the mid-fourteenth century had begun to encroach on the towns and to participate in the benefits of civilization, often returned to primitive barbarism in the uninhabitable mountains: a Serb writer of our times claims to have discovered, in completely out of the way places, poor mountaineers who did not know of sugar, taking it to be snow. The old trading routes had become extremely difficult, and soon the merchants would abandon them almost completely: the last itineraries that we have conserved date from the sixteenth century, and the last more extensive description of coastal Albania is that of Marino Bizzi, bishop of Antivari, who visited this country in 1610.

The situation of the Orthodox bishops, less suspected because of the relations which existed between the Greek element and the Turkish master, was very much better. However it worsened during the sixteenth century and above all towards the end of this century, when the new crusade launched by Pope Clement VIII, who incited into combat the Imperials of Rodolphe II, the prince of Transylvania, Sigismond Bathory, heir in his own illusions to the great King of Hungary, Matthias, the princes of Moldavia and Wallachia, of which the first, Michael the Brave, had secret relations with the Albanians, and the Cossacks, rendering suspect all Christian elements subject to the Sultan.

Even before this we see bishops from Ochrida, as prelates who bore the title of the Serb patriarchy of Ipek, leave their homeland to ask Westerners, of the German Empire, as well as Italy, and much later the Tsar of Moscow, for monetary aid and a little attention to the sufferings of their people or only of their Church.

One of these bishops of Ochrida calls himself in his requests: "Archbishop of Prima Justiniana, of all Bulgaria, Patriarch of Serbia, Macedonia, Moldova and Wallachia."

As far as local revolts are concerned in this unstable era, one Grdan Voevode led a movement in 1580; we do not know the name of the Albanian chieftains who addressed Michael the Brave to offer to support him in a war of Christian recuperation, as in times previous the young Scanderbeg offered himself to another great Romanian, John Hunyadi. But at this time the constant adversary of the same prince Michael, disputing with him the possession of Transylvania, of which he wished himself to be governor, and who, even after a formal reconciliation, pursued a vendetta against his brother in arms in the service of the emperor, was George Basta, one of those Albanians established in the Kingdom of Naples. Employed also in the Netherlands, where he had learned the art of preparing an ambush, this general, remembered as having responsibility for one of the greatest political crimes of his epoch, was among the best known military leaders and at the same time a remarkable writer in the military field and the author of memoirs published by the Italian Ciro Spontoni under the title *History of Transylvania*.

X
ALBANIA IN THE SERVICE OF THE TURKS

On the one hand then, Grdan and the unknown leaders of the revolt against the Turks, and on the other, Basta, general in the service of the German emperor, and facing these representatives of the Albanian race the generals that this same race gave at the end of the sixteenth century to the Ottoman Empire itself, like the Grands-Viziers, rivals amongst themselves, according to the custom of their nation, Ferhad and Sinan. The latter above all played a very great role, and it was him who de facto led the Ottoman Empire and had led, under Selim II, the Serb Mohammed Socoli, under the reign of the degenerate Sultans, Mourad II and Mohammed III. The eruption of this war against the Imperials in 1593 can be attributed to the ferocious energy of Sinan, his fanatical hatred of Christians, and his hope of being able to establish on the Danube Turkish pashas instead of the unreliable or rebellious Romanian princes, leading to his use in such a complete manner of the forces of an empire whose inner weakness and hidden vices were not suspected by this fervent propagator of the warrior spirit.

At the beginning of the seventeenth century the elements of leadership and civilization appeared totally lacking in the Albanian nation. The Turks, after the lesson given to them by the recent agitations during the war against the Imperials, no longer admitted most of the bishops coming from the neighboring possessions. (From 1570, it was proposed to nominate a bishop of Albanian race, subject to the Sultan and residing in Alessio.) The former episcopal seats were vacant, except perhaps that of Sopoto *(épiscopatus sopotens)* and the former "bishopric of Albania" *(episcopatus albanensis).* The Catholic religion was represented rather by Franciscan monks, in relation with those of Bosnia and Bulgaria, whose influence also extended beyond the Danube. They were at the same time political propagandists, and one of them, Francesco Antonio Bertuccio, sent to Rome and elsewhere briefings to show that it was possible to deliver Albania by means of his creation.

But the old clan life was maintained, despite this lack of organization and leadership, even at this time, which was the most unhappy, with its assemblies of the people, of which the Albanian name comes from the Latin *conventus*, with its former "judges" who, after having been *cnezes*, counts, were now, in the Turkish fashion "bannerets" of the baïraktars. We even surprisingly see old historic names returning to the surface, as with the Doucachines and the Topias. The Pastrovitsch, who also often appear in the medieval sources, play an important role. This is also the time when the importance is often stressed of the Catholic clan of the Clementi on the Adriatic Sea, near Podgoritza.

But nobody thought of revolt any longer. Those who had demonstrated for the old freedom had suffered the fate of that unhappy Albanian who was paraded through the streets of Constantinople after having been burned alive. We no longer encounter in the West, apart from the bishops we have noted, these adventurers of the late sixteenth century, such as Jean André "Angelus Flavius Comnenus, duke of Drivasto and Durazzou". It seems however that the Albanians were not strangers to this movement of deliverance of the Bulgars who, speaking of the former "lion" of their race, addressed Matthew, Prince of Wallachia, to ask him to put himself at the head of a great liberation movement.

This was the age of the Keuprulis, of which the first, this terrible old man Mohammed-Pasha, who brought order to the Empire and imposed upon it a policy of redemptive energy, was born in Asia Minor, of Albanian parents. A Moldavian chronical relates the emergence, more or less exactly reported, of Mohammed with that of another Albanian, this one Christian, who was destined to have a brilliant career: this Ghica, who would later be called Georges Ghica, when, having long been one of the main boyars of Moldavia, he obtained the throne of the country, which was granted to him through the support of the old Keupruli.

Under these Keupruli, the Albanians obtained a great role in the new Ottoman army where, instead of spahis, without military value, and the degenerate and turbulent janissaries, there appeared special bodies or provincial contingents, among which those from Albania played a principal role. The whole future of the Muslim Albanians, who completely supplanted the others, was henceforth determined by this military preparation in the legions, once more victorious, of the Albanian Keuprulis.

A new Christian offensive would lead however, before the end of the seventeenth century, to essential changes in the life of the Ottoman Empire and its peoples, of which the Albanians were not the last to reap the consequences. Nearly one hundred years after the offensive of the Albanian Sinan, the Imperials of Leopold 1st, responding to the attack against Vienna, in 1683, of the Grand-Vizier Cara-Mus-

tafa, heir of the Keuprulis, began an offensive, which, through a re-
conquered Hungary, led them beyond the Sava, in Serbia, while the
Austrian cavalry corps penetrated Bosnia and the old Albanian territories. The Christian "liberators" naturally met the opposition of the
Muslim begs of these districts. The population of the same religion,
at the head of which they found themselves, had perceptibly extended
in recent times in the direction of Old Serbia, the Serbs being in part
exhausted by the increasingly weighing regime, of a declining and
impoverished Turkey in part drawn towards the North even before
the attempts at colonization by the Austrians. It was at this time that
Muslim Albanians would colonize the villages of the coast of Prizrend, Diacovo and Ipec. As the Serb population, compromised by the
welcome it had given to the Imperials, had to leave its habitations to
settle in the lands of the Empire, to the North of the Sava and Danube (in the Banat) — it is in vain that an attempt to deny this fact
has recently been made (Iovao Tomitch, *L'Albanais en Vieille-Ser-
bie, etc.*, Paris 1916) — the Albanians could extend still further into
these new territories of their habitation.

With the outbreak of the new war between Austrians and Turks,
in 1737, the Albanian districts were again invaded. After a preparation of the inhabitants by the actions of the archbishop of Skoplié, an
Albanian this time, several Catholic clans, the Clementi, the Hoti and
so on, rose up to welcome the invading army. But the Imperials were
not in a position to support this rebellious population against the
Turks, and the repression, in which Albanian Muslims also participated, was especially cruel.

At the same time as the first war between Austrians and Turks,
Venice, allied with the Emperor in the grand Christian league, had

undertaken to reconquer the Morea. It realized this intention, and at the same time Venetian troops seized Valona and Canina on the Albanian coast. For their part, the Muslim Albanians of Scutari, under the leadership of Sanjak Soliman, belonging to the subsequently famous line of the Bouchatlia, fought, between 1685 and 1692, against the Venetians' Montenegrin allies and against the Venetian contingent itself, which was mingled with the troops of the prince-bishop. After the conclusion of a peace in 1699, which temporarily abandoned the Morea to its former Christian masters. Another Pasha of Scutari, this time a Turk, subdued Scutari, Dulcigno and Antivari, which had rebelled, as well as the Catholic Clementi tribe, which fiercely resisted. Some of these unfortunate Albanians would find a refuge on the frontiers of Austria, near Mitrovitza. A little later, in 1744, other Albanians, from Epirus, from the environs of Chimaira, settled in the south of Italy, near their brothers who had left the common homeland at the time of Scanderbeg.

During the wars the Turks were forced to fight against the Russians, in the second half of the eighteenth century, Muslim Albanians played an important role. As for their Christian brethren, we find them already at least from around 1760 in the service of the princes of Wallachia and Moldavia, and during the war that began in 1788, they came to an understanding with the Russians and formed a company in the service of the Empress Catherine. The custom of entering in the guard of the Danubian princes was maintained later also, and, when the Greeks, inspired by the ideas of the French Revolution, formed the "hétairie" which would lead the revolution of 1822, among the first initiates were found the commander of the "Arnautes" of Bucharest, the captain Georgakis or Iordachi, originally from one of the Romanian villages of the Pindus. Iordachi, like his comrade Pharmakis, was among the most valiant fighters in the movement which broke out in Moldavia; he perished in the ruins of the monastery of Secur whose bell tower he had blown up, preferring death to Turkish captivity.

Other Albanians were involved in the Napoleonic wars, which also affected the Balkan peninsula: there was an entire regiment of Albanians in the French army between 1807 and 1814. Napoleon was preoccupied with Albania, whose fate he had fixed in his projects of remodeling of the Turkish East.

But Albanian energy was demonstrated above all, as might be expected, among the Muslim Albanians. Such as the family of the Bouchatlia, already mentioned above. Pasha Cara-Mahmoud, who belonged to this family, attacked the Montenegrins between 1787 and 1796; after burning Cetinje, he was killed in an encounter with these Slav mountaineers: Jirecek tells us that his head is still conserved in the capital of Montenegro. His relative, Noustafa, would play a role in another war between Turks and Russians, in 1829, subsequently being pursued as a rebel and exiled in Asia Minor.

At the time when the son of an Albanian tobacco merchant from Cavala became viceroy of Egypt and founder of a dynasty which still exists, another representative of Muslim Albania, Ali-Pasha, obtained a quasi-royal situation in the pashalik of Janina, which he had won through his qualities and intrigues. In the history of the Ottoman empire there was never anyone who compared to this Tosk from Tepelini in combining the most ferocious energy, the most absolute contempt for human life, the most insatiable avidity and the most refined perfidy with a very high intelligence, a superior talent for handling men and a real sense of the needs of a new civilization for the peoples of a decadent Empire. He employed his relations with Constantinople, which he maintained by lavish presents, to obtain offices, like that of the governor of Rumelia, against the devastating bands of brigands, only with the aim of expanding, in Albania itself until Arta, in Macedonia until Monastir, and if possible, in Thessaly, where he had been Pasha of Tricala and where he had ensured situations to his sons, his possessions, that he believed he could found together in a new state capable of progress.

He neglected nothing in maintaining his relations with the West, and forcibly or voluntarily, he retained foreigners, "Franks," to train his troops, serve his artillery and maintain his diplomatic relations, presenting himself as a great reformer, in the European sense, of his provinces. There was undoubtedly in the tyrant of Janina, who will never be forgotten, for his cruelties as for the grandeur and pomp of his regime, something which recalls Scanderbeg himself and the whole long series of Albanian chieftains whose mission in the Balkans appeared to be that of conserving a place for the West in the peninsula.

The Greek revolution was encouraged by him. He probably hoped to take advantage of this national movement, as he had taken advantage of everything that happened in his neighborhood and sphere of influence. But the Greeks pursued their own goals, and Ali, compromised by his relations with the revolutionaries, expiated his errors rather than his crimes under the blows of assassins in the pay of the Porte during the siege of Janina, undertaken against him in 1822.

This tragic incident of Ali-Pasha was not the sole manifestation of Albanians during the Greek revolution: without counting the contingents supplied by Albania to the Turks during their vain work of repression, we should recall that among the main representatives of the Christian cause, who tended towards re-establishing the Byzantine empire, there were many Albanian chieftains, as well as the Romanians of the Pindus, and that among the hardy pirate who dared to attack the Turkish and Egyptian fleet from their fire ships there were Albanians from the islands of Hydra and Psara.

The new kingdom of Greece also had an Albanian population in the island of Egine near Athens. The Albanian element has a place that national concerns have striven to diminish as much as possible, in the population of Greece, as it was formed by the London Convention in 1830.

The Albanians remaining in Albania were only distinguished by their opposition to the "modern" reforms of Sultan Mahmoud: like the movement of 1833 in Scutari, or that of 1735, on another point of the region, or finally the uprising of the Mirdites under their "*prenc*", Bib-Doda. Later, Abdul-Hamid provoked a revolt of Albanians against the prescriptions of the treaty of Berlin, which detached a part of their country to reunite it with Montenegro (1878-1881). Henceforth the suspicious Sultan only surrounded himself with soldiers belonging to the Albanian guard, whose important role is known.

XI
ALBANIAN RENEWAL

We will not linger over the most recent uprisings in Albania in a book whose purpose is mainly to show the mission that the Albanian race fulfils - most often with the Romanians of the Pindus, their neighbors - to bring to and maintain in the Balkans the renovating influence of the Catholic and Latin West.

Because the West intervened again at this moment to give to Albanian Christians, Albanians Catholics the Scriptures, a grammar, an orthography and the first elements of a modern literature, which was certainly worth more than these violent and fleeting uprisings, in the fashion of the Middle Ages. Missionaries, like P. Bogdano (1685), had already made "observations on the language" of the Lives of the Saints. But it was not until the nineteenth century that there were works of a higher character, addressing the very soul of the old, obstinate Albania.

First of all, it is necessary to have a very special place for a Romanian lady, of very distant Albanian descent, Helene Ghica, daughter of the Vlach Ban Michel and divorced wife of a Russian prince, who, having settled in the West, devoted herself to literary studies of the most varied kind, in which she showed of an unusual erudition. She contributed, with a real sense of her consanguinity with these distant ancestors, among others, an Italian publication on the Albanians in

Romania (*Gli Albanesi in Rumania,* 1873) and another on "Albanian nationality through its popular songs" (1867).

But already, while scattered books appeared in Greek circles, as well as in Bucharest, where the Albanian colony was still flourishing, developing in the freest way in the middle of a brother people, and even in Sofia, the Albanians of Italy were beginning their activity of renewal. Among them we should cite, as translators of Western books, as editors of popular songs, as compilers of grammars and literary histories, and as original poets finally: Nicolas Camarda, Gabriel Dara, a Crispi, Giuseppe (*Memoria sulla lingua albanese,* following Leonardo Vigo's book, *Canti popolari siciliani,* Catania, 1847), Giuseppe Jubany (*Raccolta di canti popolari and rapsodie di poemi albanesi,* Trieste 1871), Giuseppe Schiro, Demetrio di Grazia, Lorecchio, Grazia, Alberto Straticu (*Manuale di letleratura albanese,* Albanian, dedicated to the Italian minister Crispi as to a fellow spirit; there is also a Romanian translation, 1890) and the poets Goffredo Ruggiero (1896) and especially Girolarao di Rada. Their work is much better than that, astonishingly, of their brothers remaining in the Balkan homeland, among whom no writer of superior talent has yet emerged: the priority of the latter was rather to give to the people the Scriptures, the books of the Church, calendars and minor literary works of imitation for the usual knowledge (like the grammar tests of Constantin Christophoridis of Elbassan). From 1886 there began the Bucharest-based publications of *Drita* (an institute of Romanian-Albanian culture existed from 1892). Later, an Albanian newspaper was published in Lausanne and another in America.

As to the political incidents which shape the brief history of the kingdom of Albania, as it was constituted in 1819 by the London conference they are too recent for us to have the necessary historical perspective. They showed the insufficiency of a government, the lack of preparation of a dominant class, the lack of orientation of a nascent civilization, which had yet to seek, with elements provided by the Albanians of Greece, by the Albanian colonies of Bucharest and so on a literary language and a proper civilization; they have shown above all what a people can suffer if they concede too easily to the partisan influences of neighbors who want nothing more than to openly or surreptitiously annex their territory; they will have proved to truly patriotic Albanians that the Austrian illusions were deceitful and shown the caution with which they must consider any foreign interference foreign which is not in relation to the memories of the country and the traditional needs of the race.

But these incidents did not provide any proof that at a time when all races are called to revival and when they are consulted themselves to declare how they intend to live in the future, one of the oldest peoples and, individually, the most talented of the European continent, do not have the same right to existence as neighbors who do not always have their great qualities.

Appendix
Extracts from Ottoman Official Statistics

Census of 1905—1906
(1. Communication from M. Berati)

1. *Sanjak* of **Novi-Bazar**:

27,980 Muslim and Turkish Albanians
19,795 Christian and Serb Albanians
<u>47,775</u> Total population

2. *Sanjak* of **Prishtina:**

254,605 Muslim Albanians
110,310 Catholic Albanians, Orthodox Albanians,
Serbs, Bulgars and Tzigane
<u>364,015</u> Total population

3. *Sanjak* of **Ipek:**

139,901 Muslim Albanians
45,878 Catholic Albanians, Orthodox Albanians
and Serbs.
<u>185,779</u> Total population

4. *Sanjak* of **Uskub:**
(The cazas of Uskub, Koumanovo and Orhanie.)

90,840 Muslim Albanians
60,706 Orthodox Albanians, Bulgars and Serbs
<u>161,545</u> Total population

5. *Sandjak* of **Prizrend:**
(The cazas of Trizrend, Kalkandelen and Goetivar)

158,742 Muslim Albanians
16,232 Catholic and Orthodox Albanians
11,602 Serbs
473 Tzigane
<u>194,480</u> Total population

6. *Vilayet* of **Monastir:**

457,994 Turkish and Muslim Albanians
264,008 Orthodox and Romanian Albanians
198,335 Bulgars.
65,108 Greeks.
7,670 Jews
2,760 Tzigane
254 Catholics and Protestants.
<u>495,732</u> Total population

7. *Vilayet* of **Janina**:

227,484 Muslim Albanians
213,281 Orthodox Albanians and Romanians
91,911 Greeks
4,906 Jews
<u>637,582</u> Total population

SUGGESTED READING

Brackob, A.K. Scanderbeg: *A History of George Castriota and the Albanian Resistance to Islamic Expansion in the Fifteenth Century*. Palm Beach: Histria Books, 2018.

Brackob, A.K. *The Formation of the Albanian National Consciousness*. Palm Beach: Histria Books, 2022

Frashëri, Kristo. *The History of Albania*. Tirana, 1964.

Nagy-Talavera, Nicholas M. *Nicolae Iorga: A Biography*. Palm Beach: Center for Romanian Studies, 2021.

Pollo, Stefanaq, and Arben Puto, *The History of Albania,* trans. Carol Wiseman and Ginnie Hole. London, 1981.

Pollo, Stefanaq. *The Proclamation of Independence of Albania- A Great Turing-Point in the History of the Albanian People*. Tirana, 1983.

Shaw, Stanford. *History of the Ottoman Empire and Modern Turkey*, Volume 2. New York, 1976.

Stavrianos, L.S. *The Balkans since 1453*. New York, 1958.

Vickers, Miranda. *The Albanians: A Modern History*. New York: I.B. Tauris, 1995.

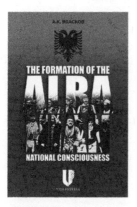